Popular Rock Superstars of Yesterday and Today

POP ROCK

AC/DC

Aerosmith

The Allman
Brothers Band

The Beatles

Billy Joel

Bob Marley
and the Wailers

Bruce Springsteen

The Doors

Elton John

The Grateful Dead

Led Zeppelin

Lynyrd Skynyrd

Pink Floyd

Queen

The Rolling
Stones

U2

The Who

Aerosmith

Ethan Schlesinger

Mason Crest Publishers

Aerosmith

FRONTIS Aerosmith—(left to right) Brad Whitford, Steven Tyler, Tom Hamilton, Joey Kramer, and Joe Perry—worked hard to earn the title "America's Band."

Produced by 21st Century Publishing and Communications, Inc.

Editorial by Harding House Publishing Services, Inc.

MASON CREST PUBLISHERS INC.
370 Reed Road
Broomall, Pennsylvania 19008
(866) MCP-BOOK (toll free)
www.masoncrest.com

Printed in the United States.

First Printing

9 8 7 6 5 4 3 2 1

Library of Congress Cataloging-in-Publication Data

Schlesinger, Ethan.
    Aerosmith / Ethan Schlesinger.
      p. cm. — (Popular rock superstars of yesterday and today)
    Includes index.
    Hardback edition: ISBN-13: 978-1-4222-0184-8
    Paperback edition: ISBN-13: 978-1-4222-0309-5
  1. Aerosmith (Musical group)—Juvenile literature. 2. Rock musicians—United States—Juvenile literature. I. Title.
ML3930.A17S35 2008
782.42166092'2—dc22   2007016931

Publisher's notes:
- All quotations in this book come from original sources, and contain the spelling and grammatical inconsistencies of the original text.

- The Web sites mentioned in this book were active at the time of publication. The publisher is not responsible for Web sites that have changed their addresses or discontinued operation since the date of publication. The publisher will review and update the Web site addresses each time the book is reprinted.

CONTENTS

ROCK 'N' ROLL TIMELINE

1951
"Rocket 88," considered by many to be the first rock single, is released by Ike Turner.

1952
DJ Alan Freed coins and popularizes the term "Rock and Roll," proclaimes himself the "Father of Rock and Roll," and declares, "Rock and Roll is a river of music that has absorbed many streams: rhythm and blues, jazz, rag time, cowboy songs, country songs, folk songs. All have contributed to the Big Beat."

1955
"Rock Around the Clock" by Bill Haley & His Comets is released; it tops the U.S. charts and becomes wildly popular in Britain, Australia, and Germany.

1969
The Woodstock Music and Arts Festival attracts a huge crowd to rural upstate New York.

1969
Tommy, the first rock opera, is released by British rock band The Who.

1967
The Monterey Pop Festival in California kicks off open air rock concerts.

1965
The psychedelic rock band, the Grateful Dead, is formed in San Francisco.

1970
The Beatles break up.

1971
Jim Morrison, lead singer of The Doors, dies in Paris.

1971
Duane Allman, lead guitarist of the Allman Brothers Band, dies.

1950s   1960s   1970s

1957
Bill Haley tours Europe.

1957
Jerry Lee Lewis and Buddy Holly become the first rock musicians to tour Australia.

1954
Elvis Presley releases the extremely popular single "That's All Right (Mama)."

1961
The first Grammy for Best Rock 'n' Roll Recording is awarded to Chubby Checker for *Let's Twist Again*.

1964
The Beatles make their first visit to America, setting off the British Invasion.

1969
A rock concert held at Altamont Speedway in California is marred by violence.

1969
The Rolling Stones tour America as "The Greatest Rock and Roll Band in the World."

1973
Rolling Stone magazine names Annie Leibovitz chief photographer and "rock 'n' roll photographer;" she follows and photographs rockers Mick Jagger, John Lennon, and others.

1974
Sheer Heart Attack by the British rock band Queen becomes an international success.

1974
"Sweet Home Alabama" by Southern rock band Lynyrd Skynyrd is released and becomes an American anthem.

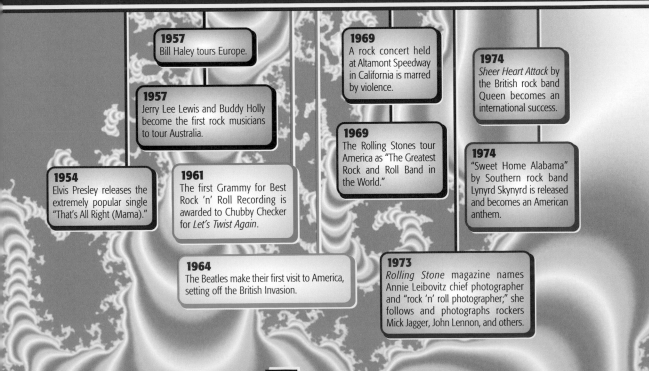

1987
Billy Joel becomes the first American rock star to perform in the Soviet Union since the construction of the Berlin Wall.

2005
Led Zeppelin is ranked #1 on VH1's list of the 100 Greatest Artists of Hard Rock.

2005
Many rock groups participate in Live 8, a series of concerts to raise awareness of extreme poverty in Africa.

1985
Rock stars perform at Live Aid, a benefit concert to raise money to fight Ethiopian famine.

2003
Led Zeppelin's "Stairway to Heaven" is inducted into the Grammy Hall of Fame.

1980
John Lennon of the Beatles is murdered in New York City.

2000s
Aerosmith's album sales reach 140 million worldwide and the group becomes the bestselling American hard rock band of all time.

2007
Billy Joel become the first person to sing the National Anthem before two Super Bowls.

1975
Tommy, the movie, is released.

1995
The Rock and Roll Hall of Fame and Museum opens in Cleveland, Ohio.

1975
Time magazine features Bruce Springsteen on its cover as "Rock's New Sensation."

1970s   1980s   1990s   2000s

1979
Pink Floyd's *The Wall* is released.

1991
Freddie Mercury, lead vocalist of the British rock group Queen, dies of AIDS.

2004
Elton John receives a Kennedy Center Honor.

1979
The first Grammy for Best Rock Vocal Performance by a Duo or Group is awarded to The Eagles.

2004
Rolling Stone Magazine ranks The Beatles #1 of the 100 Greatest Artists of All Time, and Bob Dylan #2.

1986
The Rolling Stones receive a Grammy Lifetime Achievement Award.

1981
MTV goes on the air.

2006
U2 wins five more Grammys, for a total of 22—the most of any rock artist or group.

1986
The first Rock and Roll Hall of Fame induction ceremony is held; Chuck Berry, Little Richard, Ray Charles, Elvis Presley, and James Brown, are among the first inductees.

1981
For Those About to Rock We Salute You by Australian rock band AC/DC becomes the first hard rock album to reach #1 in the U.S.

2006
Bob Dylan, at age 65, releases *Modern Times* which immediately rises to #1 in the U.S.

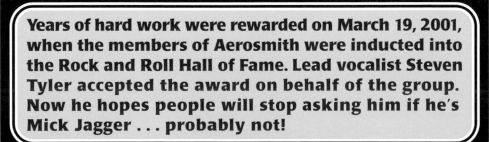

Years of hard work were rewarded on March 19, 2001, when the members of Aerosmith were inducted into the Rock and Roll Hall of Fame. Lead vocalist Steven Tyler accepted the award on behalf of the group. Now he hopes people will stop asking him if he's Mick Jagger . . . probably not!

"America's Band"

By 2001, Aerosmith had become a legend in rock music. The group had sold millions of records and CDs. It had performed in front of huge audiences all over the world. Still, on a March 2001 evening, the members of Aerosmith were overwhelmed by what was happening: they were being inducted into the Rock and Roll Hall of Fame.

That night at the Waldorf-Astoria Hotel in New York City, Aerosmith joined other music legends, including Queen, Michael Jackson, Ritchie Valens, and Solomon Burke, in perhaps the most **prestigious** honor that rock musicians can achieve. The audience in the glamorous hotel's ballroom was made up of some of the biggest names in the music industry, all there to honor the best of the best. **Induction** into the hall is not a "given." It's an honor that has to be earned.

Making It into the Hall

Like those who become members of the Baseball Hall of Fame, the Football Hall of Fame, and similar halls, membership in the Rock and Roll Hall of Fame has to be earned. Inductees must meet the tough standards the nominating committee of the Rock and Roll Hall of Fame requires just to put a musician's name on the ballot. According to Rock and Roll Hall of Fame rules, twenty-five years must have passed since a potential nominee's first recording. Those considered for nomination must have made a significant contribution to the development of rock music. Those who meet the **criteria** are placed on the ballot, which is sent to music experts all over the world. To be inducted, the nominee must have the most votes, and be selected on more than 50 percent of the ballots.

Some musicians are nominated many times before they make it into the Rock and Roll Hall of Fame, if they ever do. For other musicians, such as Aerosmith, it only takes two nominations. Whether on a first or second try, or even a seventh or eighth, most inductees are truly humbled by the honor. (The British punk group the Sex Pistols was an exception. They refused to attend the ceremony when they were inducted.)

Presented to the Hall

Each new inductee into the Rock and Roll Hall of Fame is presented by another person from the music industry. Sometimes the person is a fan; other times there is a direct connection between the inductee and the presenter. For Aerosmith, its presenter, Kid Rock, was both. He has often said that Aerosmith had been a big influence on him as a musician. During his speech, he called Aerosmith—Tom Hamilton, Joey Kramer, Joe Perry, Steven Tyler, and Brad Whitford—"the greatest rock band in American music."

During their acceptance speeches, the members of Aerosmith thanked family and friends for continuing support. Steven also mused: "I wonder if this will put an end to 'Hey, aren't you Mick Jagger?'"

As is customary at the Rock and Roll Hall of Fame induction ceremony, the evening ended with a **jam** session with many of the evening's inductees and their presenters doing what they love most—making music. This time, even members of the audience were brought onstage to participate in an unforgettable finale.

Kid Rock (right) presented Aerosmith at the group's Rock and Roll Hall of Fame ceremonies. After a speech in which he called Aerosmith "the greatest rock band in American music" and a major influence on his music career, Kid Rock joined Steven Tyler (left) and the other members of Aerosmith for a rousing jam session.

During backstage interviews after the ceremony, Steven reflected on how he felt about receiving the award and becoming a member of the Rock and Roll Hall of Fame:

"It's totally overwhelming, because when you see all these people up there that you cut your teeth on, and listened to and heard, to think that you've got a room next to Elvis Presley now, is like, wow!"

Aerosmith—"America's Band"—came to the aid of a hurting nation on October 21, 2001. The group was among those that performed at the United We Stand: What More Can I Give? benefit concert in Washington, D.C. The concert raised funds to help the victims of the terrorist attacks of September 11, 2001.

Its Rock and Roll Hall of Fame induction wasn't the only important event for the group in 2001.

America's Band

On September 11, 2001, the world changed. Terrorists hijacked four planes, intending to crash them into buildings on the East Coast of the United States. Two crashed into the Twin Towers of the World Trade Center in New York City. Another crashed into the Pentagon outside of Washington, D.C. The fourth plane crashed into the rural Pennsylvania countryside, its intended target not known with certainty. Thousands of people were killed that day. Many more were injured, physically and emotionally.

The music world came together just one month later to help those who had been most affected by the events that tragic September day. Michael Jackson, Rod Stewart, the Backstreet Boys, Bette Midler, P. Diddy, Mariah Carey, and Destiny's Child were among the musicians who performed at United We Stand: What More Can I Give: A Concert for Washington D.C. and America. Aerosmith was on its highly success-ful *Just Push Play* tour, but the band members interrupted their tour to come to Washington and participate in the concert.

After all, as Joe Perry has often remarked, "We were America's band." They started small, became almost larger than life, and then seemed to fall off a **precipice**. More important, the group had rebounded to be better than ever. And that's what America would do.

The group performed at the concert, then returned to Indianapolis, Indiana, to pick up the tour that same evening. Part of being "America's Band" was not disappointing the fans who had supported the group during its ups and downs—very high ups and very low downs. The former "bad boys from Boston" knew who was responsible for their rise from garage band to rock legends.

The members of Aerosmith proved that the American Dream was alive and well—if you were willing to work hard. The group started as a garage band, grew into one of the hottest bands in the world, and crashed—big time. But the guys got their act together and reached the top again.

Garage Band Makes It Big

Who doesn't want to be a rock star at some point in life? For teens and young adults, wanting to be a rocker seems to be a natural **rite of passage**. Well, things weren't much different in the 1960s, whether you lived in Iowa, California, Texas, or even New Hampshire.

And when the British Invasion hit the U.S. shores, well, the number of people wanting to make their mark on the music world swelled. Among those who had visions of rock superstardom were Steven Tallarico, Joe Perry, and Tom Hamilton. A dishwashing job would bring the guys together and eventually create one of the biggest names in rock history—Aerosmith.

Dishpan Hands

Steven Tallarico, who would become better known as Steven Tyler, was one of those young people hoping for a career in music. He had grown up around music; his father, Vic, had his own orchestra. During the early 1960s, Steven played drums and sang for several bands in his hometown of Yonkers, New York. The Strangeurs/Chain Reaction, Fox Chase, and William Proud were just some of the groups that had the benefit of his musical talents.

In 1969, Steven was vacationing in Sunapee, New Hampshire. Also in Sunapee were Joe Perry and Tom Hamilton, along with David "Pudge" Scott. Joe, Tom, and Pudge played in a local group called the Jam Band. Joe was also washing dishes at the Anchorage, a restaurant at Sunapee Harbor. The guys shared their love of music, but it would take a move to another state to bring forth Aerosmith.

Finally, a Group

In the fall of 1970, Joe and Tom moved to Boston, where they met Joey Kramer. Joey was a drummer, and, like Steven, hailed from Yonkers. Joey was also a music student in college, but he decided to give up on college to join Joe and Tom. The guys got in touch with Steven, who was anxious to join Joe, Tom, and Joey, but he had one condition—he wanted to sing lead, not play drums. Since Joey was already onboard, the guys agreed, and they had a band. Steven's friend Ray Tabano joined the group to play rhythm guitar.

Now all they needed was a name. It wasn't unusual for bands to play under many names before finding just the right one. This wasn't the case for Aerosmith. According to the Rock and Roll Hall of Fame:

> **"They called themselves Aerosmith, an 'imaginary band name' dreamed up and doodled on notebooks by Kramer in high school."**

In 1971, Ray left the band and was replaced by Brad Whitford, who had played with the group Earth Inc. Once Brad joined the group, the lineup of the band that would become a legend was set for many years.

The British Invasion and Aerosmith

In the 1960s, the United States had found itself invaded by a foreign power. This time, however, the purpose of the invasion was musical—not political—domination. The invading force came from Great Britain and were named the Beatles, the Who, and the Rolling Stones, among others. For a few years, British bands overtook American bands in fan popularity and record sales. Some U.S. bands found it impossible to compete against the foreign "invaders," and they gave up their dreams to make it big on the music scene.

U.S. record companies needed a way for their clients to compete with the British groups. For many groups, that meant changing their sound to include some of the stylistic qualities of the British groups who were making a killing on album sales in the United States.

In the 1960s there was no group hotter than the Beatles. Ringo Starr, George Harrison, Paul McCartney, and John Lennon (left to right) led the British Invasion of the United States. They also spawned dreams of becoming rock superstars in teens and young adults—talented or not—all across the country.

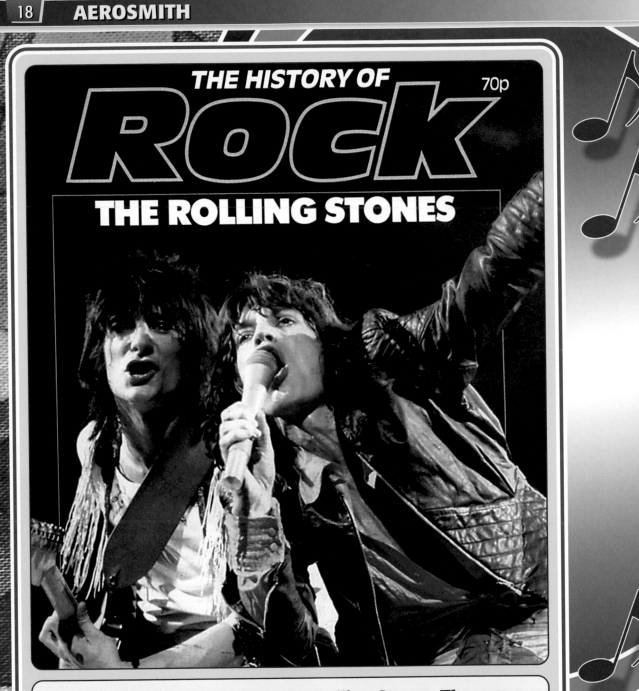

THE HISTORY OF
ROCK

70p

THE ROLLING STONES

Other British Invaders were the Rolling Stones. The group was extremely popular in the United States, and many other groups tried to imitate the band. Some critics believed that was what Aerosmith was trying to do and dismissed the guys as Rolling Stone knockoffs. It wouldn't take long before critics learned otherwise.

And this is what new groups, such as Aerosmith, also did. The bluesy quality of the British Invasion attracted the members of the group, especially Steven, who was extremely fond of the **blues**. The group and its British Invasion–influenced sound became a popular local attraction in 1971. But the guys wanted to hit the big time and felt they were ready.

A Label and an Album

Columbia Records thought Aerosmith was ready for the big time, too, and in 1972, the group signed its first record deal with the label. In 1973, the group released its debut album, *Aerosmith*. The influence of the British Invasion could not be missed on the album. In fact, several critics were quick to dismiss the group as simply a Rolling Stones wannabe. The fact that there was a physical resemblance between Stones frontman Mick Jagger and Steven added fuel to the argument.

Not everyone agreed with the criticism. According to the Rock and Roll Hall of Fame, although there was an obvious influence on the group of the bands that made up the British Invasion:

❝they [Aerosmith] were flashier and more hard-hitting than their precursors, helping to draft a new blueprint for rock music in the brave new world of the Seventies.❞

Aerosmith wasn't a huge hit at the time it was released, but eventually it would sell more than 2 million copies. The label released all but one of the songs as singles, but only one—"Dream On"—charted, though only as high as #59. It has since become one of the most favorite rock ballads in history.

The Wings to Success

Like most bands of the time, Aerosmith spent a large amount of time touring. Fans got to know the band and its sounds, and when the group's second album was released in 1974, a built-in audience was waiting for it. *Get Your Wings* was the beginning of a series of hit albums for the group. For the first time, Aerosmith had legitimate radio hits with "Same Old Song and Dance" and "S.O.S. (Too Bad)."

Get Your Wings was Aerosmith's first hit, but it was only the first of many for the "bad boys from Boston." With this album and the follow-up, *Toys in the Attic*, critics across the country who had written off the group as Rolling Stone wannabes had to eat their words.

The group followed up its 1974 release with their first real hit album, *Toys in the Attic*. It was this 1975 album that made the critics who had at first been quick to write off the group as **derivative** change their minds. The group's sound on this album expanded beyond the blues-rock of its debut. Now there were hints of

psychedelic rock, heavy metal, **punk**, and other styles along with Aerosmith's bluesy sound.

The album's "Sweet Emotion" became Aerosmith's first top-40 hit. "Walk This Way," another hit from the album, remains popular more than thirty years after its release. Aerosmith was now so popular that Columbia decided to re-release "Dream On" from the group's first album. Smart move; the song shot up the singles chart to #6! *Aerosmith* and *Get Your Wings* also found new life based on the success of *Toys*, hitting the album charts along with Aerosmith's new release.

Aerosmith again found success in 1976. *Rocks* was certified **platinum** almost immediately after its release. "Last Child," "Back in the Saddle," and "Home Tonight" were staples on FM radio stations across the country.

With the release of it third hit album, Aerosmith had become a driving force in rock music. The Rock and Roll Hall of Fame describes *Wings, Toys*, and *Rocks* as

"three strong albums of genre-defining rock music. . . . that established them [Aerosmith] as America's band in the Seventies."

Groups like Guns N'Roses, Metallica, and Mötley Crüe cite *Toys* and *Rocks* as major influences on their music.

Aerosmith was a huge hit with fans, and its music had grabbed the attention of the world. They were on top and intended to stay there. Don't they all . . .

By the late 1970s, Aerosmith was one of the hottest bands in the country and in the world. The guys worked hard and they played hard. Steven and Joe partied *very* hard. Before long, it looked as though the hard living and hard partying might doom what Joey, Tom, Brad, Steven, and Joe had worked so hard to achieve.

Rockin' Hard—
to the End?

By 1976, Joe, Steven, Joey, Tom, and Brad had found the key to rock success. The band worked hard inside and outside the studio. In April 1976, Aerosmith began its first headlining tour. In February 1977, the group toured Japan for the first time. Aerosmith had found success not only in the United States, but worldwide.

Fans loved the sound, and they loved Steven's lyrics. Aerosmith's song lyrics frequently included jokes and **double entendres**, making the fans feel as though they were part of a special inner circle. It wasn't long before the band rivaled—and often surpassed—in popularity such legends as KISS and Led Zeppelin.

By the mid-1970s, music in the United States was beginning to change. Disco was becoming more popular, and some bands felt the effect of the changing tide of music. But not Aerosmith; the group knew how to hold onto its fans. Joe reflected on this ability several years later:

> **"We do what we want to do. Like back in '76, when they said 'Rock 'n' roll is dead, disco is here to stay', we were giving everybody the finger. We were selling out and selling more records than anybody . . . we play for the people."**

Arena Rock

Aerosmith's 's increasing success meant they had to play in larger and larger **venues**. The band became one of the biggest in arena rock. Sometimes called stadium rock or anthem rock, arena rock is not as clearly defined as other "styles" of rock. Over time, it has come to mean hard rock that features the guitar and keyboards played by superstar groups, bands so popular they need very large venues to accommodate their fans.

Music historians trace the first arena rock performances to the late 1960s and the British Invasion, especially the Beatles and the Rolling Stones. They often date arena rock concerts from the 1965 Beatles concert at Shea Stadium in New York City.

During the 1970s and early 1980s, arena rock featured a "softer" hard rock. It wasn't quite heavy metal, but it certainly wasn't adult contemporary either! Some of the bands who became known as arena rock bands were Queen, Journey, Kansas, Styx, Survivor, and of course, Aerosmith.

In the 1970s and 1980s, bands considered arena rock didn't need the big stadiums just for the huge numbers of fans who came to the concerts. Some of the groups, such as Queen, put on really big shows, with monstrously sized sets and equipment. There was no way the equipment and stage sets could fit into the smaller, more intimate clubs and halls that had been important in the early days of rock.

The "Toxic Twins"

Joe, Steven, Brad, Tom, and Joey went back into the recording studio in 1977. This time, however, the result, *Draw the Line*, was a disappointment.

Aerosmith got so popular that ordinary clubs and forums could not hold everyone who wanted to experience an Aerosmith performance. The band had to hold its concerts in giant sports stadiums and arenas. In the 1970s and 1980s, Aerosmith concerts were some of the biggest in arena rock, often outselling groups such as Queen, Styx, and Journey.

Critics weren't crazy about the album, and the group's fans didn't rush to buy it. "Kings and Queens" did achieve some success, however.

The reason for the album's lack of success could be traced to a hobby Joe and Steven shared—taking drugs, especially stimulants and heroin. Drug use was on the rise during the 1970s, and not just among members of rock bands. Aerosmith was one of the bands best known for its drug-abusing lifestyle. Joe's and Steven's drug and alcohol abuse and bad behavior became the stuff of legends, causing many in the

Steven's (left) and Joe's (right) talents could not be denied. But sometimes it seemed as though the dynamic duo was bent on self-destruction. Those were the times it seemed as if they were trying to see who could do more drugs or drink more alcohol. Their lifestyle earned the pair the nickname the "Toxic Twins."

music press to refer to the duo as the "Toxic Twins." They were like spoiled kids who had gotten their own way too many times.

According to Steven:

> **"I can remember the height of my oblivion, when I was doing things just because I could. I would think nothing of tipping over a table with a whole long spread on it just because there was a turkey roll on the table and I had explicitly said, 'No turkey roll.'"**

Joe recalled the excesses made available by the group's success:

> **"We get to L.A., everybody is staying in Century City but us [Joe and Steven]. We're at the Beverly Hills Hotel with a liquor tab of $5,000 because all the bands are coming over from Century City and partying all night with us. The waiters were in a bucket brigade. We were on the phone with room service every twelve minutes. It was great. All we had to do was say what we wanted, and that was it."**

Joe's and Steven's drug use wasn't limited to offstage. Steven was known for wrapping a scarf around the mic stand. Sometimes it was just for show, but other times—perhaps most of the time—the scarf hid his substance of choice for the evening, which he would partake of during the performance.

A Tour and a Film

In June 1977, Aerosmith began its *Draw the Line* tour, which lasted into 1978. One stop on the tour was as headliner at Texas Jam '78 Festival on July 4, 1978. Though the album hadn't been a big hit, the group's concert tour was. And Aerosmith wasn't the only draw to the concerts. Concert-goers were treated to such opening musicians as AC/DC and Ted Nugent.

Aerosmith also expanded into another area in the late 1970s. In 1978, the Beatles decided to make a film, *Sgt. Pepper's Lonely Heart's Club Band*. The Beatles were beginning to fade into rock history by the late 1970s, and some music historians view the film as a last-ditch effort to reclaim some of their past glory days.

In *Sgt. Pepper's Lonely Heart's Club Band*, Joe, Steven, Brad, Tom, and Joey played members of the Future Villain Band. Any hopes the Beatles might have had that the film would jump-start their waning career were quickly dashed. Critics panned the film, and it was a financial flop as well. Despite that, the members of Aerosmith escaped the wrath of the critics, and its music career was not marred. In fact, its cover of the Beatles hit "Come Together," featured in the film, was a big hit. Reaching #23 on the *Billboard* singles chart, "Come Together" was the last time Aerosmith hit the top-40 for the next decade.

On the Downslide

Eventually, the group's lifestyle of partying, drug and alcohol abuse, and excesses began to take a toll on its music. Hints of what was to come had begun with *Draw the Line*. The album was late because of Joe's and Steven's substance abuse problems; sometimes Joe and Steven were too strung out to work, or at least to produce quality music.

In 1978, Aerosmith released a live album, *Live! Bootleg*. Many of the tracks on the album were recorded during the *Draw the Line* tour. It reminded fans and critics of the Aerosmith of old, and the double album was generally met favorably by both fans and critics.

The release of *Live! Bootleg* was followed by another Aerosmith tour. On October 3, 1978, Aerosmith bailed out fifty-three fans who had been arrested for smoking marijuana at the Fort Wayne, Indiana, concert stop. Just a week later, Joe and Steven received minor injuries when a fan threw a cherry bomb onto the stage at the Philadelphia show. The tour was nothing if not interesting.

Good-Bye Joe

After the tour, Joe, Steven, Tom, Joey, and Brad were back in the recording studio. By now, the effects of drug and alcohol abuse were apparent in the work product of all the group's members. But it wasn't just substance abuse that affected Aerosmith's next album, *Night in the Ruts*. The group had toured and recorded almost constantly since hitting the big time in 1973. One tour would end, the group would go into the studio and record another album, and the next tour would begin. The guys had little down time. On top of the drug abuse, they were tired, and it showed.

Steven did not limit his drug and alcohol use to offstage activities. During performances, his long scarves, often tied to microphone stands, became his signature. What many fans did not know at the time was that sometimes the scarves hid a flask or drugs, from which Steven would partake during a performance.

Not long after *Night in the Ruts* was released in 1979, Joe left the group. Only Joe and perhaps the other members of the band know the real reason Joe left. Officially, the reason given when Joe's departure was announced was the often-used phrase "creative differences." Some claim that it was constant fighting, often drug induced, between Joe and Steven. Others claim jealousy; Steven was more devoted to the group and resented Joe's lack of dedication, his seemingly greater interest in women than in the group. Still others believe that it was a

In 1979, Joe left the group. Though the reason given for the sudden departure was "creative differences," some people speculate that it was really the almost-constant fighting between Joe and Steven. Others believe the real reason was jealousy. Others suggest that a fight between girlfriends led to the split. No one except those involved know the real reason.

major tiff between Joe's and Steven's girlfriends that prompted Joe to leave Aerosmith and form his own band, the Joe Perry Project. Regardless of the why, the fact was that for the first time since its creation, Aerosmith needed a new member.

Going On

When Joe left the group, he was replaced by Richie Supa. Richie had known the band members for many years, and most considered him a friend, as well as a talented songwriter. But before the tour supporting the new album began, Richie was replaced by Jimmy Crespo, who had played with the group Flame.

Again Aerosmith found itself touring to support an album that wasn't successful. *Night in the Ruts* was even less successful than *Draw the Line* of 1977. Both the album's sales and the tour were disappointing.

Not everything looked bleak for the members of Aerosmith after Joe's departure, though. In 1980, *Greatest Hits* was released, and the group again found commercial success. But things would again turn sour when Steven was seriously injured in a motorcycle accident in the summer. He spent months in the hospital recuperating from his injuries. The accident reportedly involved the use of both drugs and alcohol.

With Steven recuperating, the group had some down time. But things did not get better. After Brad laid down guitar tracks for "Lightning Strikes," a song for the next album, he decided he wanted to leave Aerosmith. Once again the group found itself without one of its original members, one of the guys who had worked hard to make the group a legend. Brad was replaced by guitarist Rick Dufay.

After Brad's departure in 1981, many in the music industry were wondering whether Aerosmith could go on. There was no question that, except for the *Greatest Hits* album, record sales were drastically down. Concert attendance was down as well. The group no longer needed vast stadiums or arenas for concert performances; clubs would do just fine. Perhaps it was time for Aerosmith to fade into rock history.

With members coming and going, and a recent history of lackluster sales, some people wondered if the band that had been so hot in the 1970s would completely crash and burn in the 1980s. But while the decade got off to a rocky start, the band members would prove they weren't ready for the rock 'n' roll retirement home just yet.

4

Resurrection

Oh how the mighty had fallen. Aerosmith had reached the top, but then seemed to plummet to a splat. The only way the group seemed able to get a hit was to release previously recorded material. Steven, Joey, and Tom weren't ready to give up, though, and with Rick and Jimmy settled into the group, Aerosmith kept plugging on.

In 1982, the newest form of Aerosmith released its first album, *Rock in a Hard Place*. The album didn't do particularly well, failing to crack the top-10 on *Billboard*'s album charts. Compared to the group's other albums, *Rock in a Hard Place* failed commercially; it only reached gold status, meaning it sold 500,000 copies, rather than the platinum ranking, signifying one million copies sold, the band was used to. None of the singles released from the album reached hit status. But the album and the supporting tour weren't complete failures.

of the 1980s. *Classics Live I* and *Classics Live II*, which featured Aerosmith's reunion tour, and *Gems* all made money for Columbia.

In 1985, Aerosmith released its first album as a reunited rock legend. *Done with Mirrors* was fairly popular with fans, but it didn't really put the group back on the rock map. None of the album's singles were hits.

Steven and Joe also accomplished something else in 1985, something that benefited *every* aspect of their lives—they got clean.

Getting Clean

Drugs and alcohol had been prevalent almost since Aerosmith began. Steven had been addicted to heroin for many years, and its effects on his health were obvious. He even collapsed onstage in the early 1980s due to the effects of drugs. Both Steven and Joe, along with other members of Aerosmith, also drank heavily.

After *Done with Mirrors* was released, Joe and Steven went into rehab to get clean. And it wasn't easy. Still, Joe and Steven persevered, working hard on recovery. Once clean, they were able to see what effects the years of substance abuse had had on them and those around them. According to Steven, "Four rehabilitation centers for drug abuse later, I've been able to take a long, hard look at my behavior."

In an interview on the Web site www.superseventies.com, Steven describes his experience as an alcoholic and rock star:

> **"But I was just so selfish and one-sided. I would crawl into a little hole with whatever drug I was doing, and that's how I lived. It was OK to be drinking away my life. The manager would come backstage and say, 'Fine. Drink all you want. Just go onstage.' That was great for an alcoholic to hear. It was the perfect place to be. Liquor flowed backstage. Someone would say, 'Give him what he wants from the bar.'"**

In another interview, he talks about not remembering the band's success of the 1970s: "We call them 'The Wonder Years,' because we wonder what happened to them."

On the www.superseventies.com Web site, Joe describes the effects of alcohol and drugs on the band and its music:

"So we drank to keep the vibe we felt. It was like, if we feel good, maybe the audience will feel good. If we're getting off on the music we're playing, maybe they'll get off on it. Of course, if you listen to our records down through the years, it definitely gets diluted. We started to lose sight of it, we started to see how screwed up we could get before we walked onstage, just to see if we could get away

Steven Tyler is no dummy. After collapsing onstage and experiencing other drug-related health problems, Steven knew he had to get clean. But he soon found it was not going to be easy. In fact, it took Steven four stints in rehab until he was able to get clean. But the important thing is that he *did* get sober.

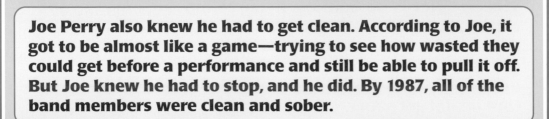

Joe Perry also knew he had to get clean. According to Joe, it got to be almost like a game—trying to see how wasted they could get before a performance and still be able to pull it off. But Joe knew he had to stop, and he did. By 1987, all of the band members were clean and sober.

with it. There were times when we were on our knees, literally, trying to find blow. There were times when we would drink just to see how much we could consume. . . . It did suffer in the end, that little picture, that little window to what we thought we were all about. "

After Joe and Steven went through rehab, the other members of the band got clean as well. By 1987, all of the band members had successfully completed rehab programs. For a while, the group even had its employees sign contracts vowing they wouldn't drink alcohol, even on days they were off. The employees fought the requirement, and the group eventually did away with it.

Climbing to the Top

In 1986, Run-DMC was one of the hottest groups in hip-hop, and the band members—Joseph "DJ Run" Simmons, Darryl "D.M.C." McDaniels, and Jason "Jam Master Jay" Mizell—wanted to **cover** Aerosmith's big 1975 hit "Walk This Way." Now drug and alcohol free, Steven and Joe sang on the track, which became the first hip-hop song to crack *Billboard*'s top-10 singles charts when it hit #4. They also appeared on the video for the song. Aerosmith found itself with new fans as a result of this blending of music styles.

Permanent Vacation was released in 1987 and became the group's best-selling album in a decade. The album produced the hit singles "Dude (Looks Like a Lady)," "Angel," and "Rag Doll"; all cracked *Billboard*'s top-20 singles charts. The group followed the album with the *Permanent Vacation* tour, which lasted for almost a year. For many dates on the tour, Guns N'Roses opened for Aerosmith. Touring with Guns N'Roses was challenging for the newly sober Aerosmith members. Drugs and alcohol played big roles in the lives of the members of Guns N'Roses, as they once had for the guys of Aerosmith. The tour was very successful, but it was not without tension between the two bands.

Back to the Top

Aerosmith's next album, *Pump*, was a hit with fans and critics alike. The album spun off three top-10 singles and brought the group its first Grammy win when "Janie's Got a Gun" won for Best Rock Performance by a Duo or Group with Vocal.

The band went on an international tour in support of *Pump*. After the tour, Aerosmith took a break so the guys could relax and spend time with their families. But they were back in the studio in 1993, and the result was *Get a Grip*, Aerosmith's first album to debut at #1 on the album charts. Fans loved the album, but critics weren't sure. Some accused the group of selling out for commercial success.

Success quickly found the now-sober Aerosmith. The guys worked hard to get new fans, and it worked. Steve and Joe recorded with Run D.M.C. The band performed on *Saturday Night Live*. And Aerosmith videos were hot on MTV. In this photo, Steven (left) and Joe (right) pose at the MTV Video Music Awards in 1987.

By the end of the decade, Aerosmith was again at the top of its game. The group had hit records and incredibly successful tours. The group's "old" fans had stuck with the guys during the group's less than successful years, and they were there in full force with the rejuvenated Aerosmith.

Some reviewers called the ballads on the album "interchangeable." But the fans were not to be denied, and they were huge hits on MTV. The actress Alicia Silverstone appeared in so many of Aerosmith's videos for the album that she earned the nickname "the Aerosmith chick." *Get a Grip* also brought the group two more Grammy Awards, one at the 36th Grammy Awards for Best Rock Performance by a Duo or Group with Vocal for "Livin' on the Edge," and another at the 37th Grammy Awards for Best Rock Performance by a Duo or Group with Vocal for "Crazy."

As the century ended, the members of Aerosmith had a lot of which to be proud. They had survived a split, accidents, and drug and alcohol addiction to end the twentieth century at the top. The group's hard work was rewarded with Grammy Awards in 1999. Tom, Brad, Steven, Joey, and Joe (from left) pose here with their statues.

By the 1990s, Aerosmith had been performing as a group for twenty years. New groups—with younger members—were forming and gaining on Aerosmith's popularity. But rather than give up, the members of Aerosmith became experts at self-promotion. They toured for eighteen months in support of *Get a Grip*. They appeared on *Saturday Night Live*. They performed songs in the hit film *Wayne's World 2*. They performed at Woodstock '94. They even opened their own club, Mama Kin's Music Hall in Boston, where the last performance of the *Get a Grip* tour was broadcast live on radio.

Closing in on the End of a Century

As the 1990s came to a close, Aerosmith appeared to be riding a high—without the use of drugs or alcohol. The group took another brief vacation, and refreshed, in 1997 the guys worked on *Nine Lives*. Things didn't go smoothly for that album. First, the group fired its manager; band members claim he almost caused the group to break up when he constantly prodded the guys to work when they really needed to rest. Then, the group decided the album needed a new producer.

Nine Lives received lukewarm reviews from the critics. After an initial surge in sales, fan response to the album drastically fell off. It did manage to stay on the charts for a long time, and eventually was certified platinum. The *Nine Lives* tour lasted for more than two years. Dates had to be postponed because of injuries suffered by Steven (he injured his leg during a performance) and Joey (who was burned when his car exploded at a gas station; no one ever said being a rock star wasn't hard). The album also brought Aerosmith another Grammy when "Pink" won for Best Rock Performance by a Duo or Group with Vocal.

In 1998, Aerosmith had one of its biggest hits ever, "I Don't Want to Miss a Thing," recorded for the soundtrack of the film *Armageddon*. The movie starred Bruce Willis, Billy Bob Thornton, Ben Affleck, and Steven's daughter Liv. Again the group found itself with a new set of fans—and an Academy Award nomination (though they wouldn't win).

In 1999, Aerosmith became an amusement park ride . . . well, kind of. The group provided the soundtrack and theme for the Disney ride Rock 'n' Roller Coaster Starring Aerosmith. Now that was an honor few other bands could claim!

With the close of the century, Aerosmith was still popular. The band had proved that it was possible to hit bottom and rise again to the top. It took time, hard work, and talent. The trick would now be to see if it could *stay* on top, or at least relevant on the music scene.

How is it possible that a group made up of men in their forties and fifties could still be on top of the rock world? If the group is Aerosmith, talent plays a big part in keeping it hot. But so is the guys' willingness to tackle new projects, ones that introduce them to new fans.

New Century– Continued Success

One of the top groups as the twentieth century changed to the twenty-first was made up of men in their late forties or early fifties. Despite the age difference between members and fans, Aerosmith had learned during the 1990s how to keep its finger on the pulse of the music scene.

The group never hesitated to take on projects that could bring them new fans. Whether it was participating in the creation of an amusement park ride or performing live with Run DMC and Kid Rock at the MTV Video Music Awards, Joe, Steven, Tom, Brad, and Joey knew how to keep the fans interested.

The Super Bowl

In January of 2001, Aerosmith played during the halftime show of Super Bowl XXXV. Other rockers playing in the show were *N Sync, Britney Spears, Mary J. Blige, and Nelly. For the finale, they joined Aerosmith for a rousing rendition of the group's classic "Walk This Way." The crowd roared its approval; the band members might be getting older, but their music was as "today" as that of any group on the rock scene.

Just Push Play

Aerosmith was also back in the recording studio in 2001. *Just Push Play*, released in March, was one of the group's biggest hits. Not long after its release, the album sold one million copies, making it another platinum release for the group. "Jaded," a single from the album, cracked the *Billboard* top-10 singles charts at #7. The title track was featured on commercials for Dodge. Most people saw this as harmless, but some critics voiced concern that the group was selling out just to make money.

The *Just Push Play* tour was another success for the group. The tour played to packed venues in the United States and Japan, though three concerts were canceled as a result of the terrorist attacks of September 11, 2001. When Michael Jackson put out the word that he was organizing the United We Stand: What More Can I Give concert to benefit those who had lost relatives in the terrorist attacks, Aerosmith was eager to participate. The concert was scheduled for Sunday, October 21. Aerosmith was scheduled to play a concert at Conseco Fieldhouse in Indianapolis that evening. Something as simple as a scheduling conflict was not about to keep Aerosmith away from the benefit concert in the nation's capital. After all, Aerosmith was America's Band. So, the guys played the concert in Washington, then hopped a plane to return to Indianapolis for the *Just Push Play* performance—all without missing a beat.

The Hall of Fame

Aerosmith's reached what some call the pinnacle of success with its induction into the Rock and Roll Hall of Fame in 2001. Within the futuristic-looking building on the shore of Lake Erie are tributes to Aerosmith, including photos and memorabilia from the group's decades of contributions to rock music.

Just Push Play **was a tremendous hit for Aerosmith in 2001. The album quickly reached platinum status. The group's** *Just Push Play* **tour played to packed stadiums across the country and Japan. Not bad for a band that just a few years ago had been back to playing small concert halls and clubs.**

In describing Aerosmith, the Rock and Roll Hall of Fame reports:

"No group in rock history has ever engineered a Phoenix-like resurrection to rival Aerosmith's remarkable recovery and rebound. Remarkably, their chart success from 1987 onward eclipsed their first rise to the top in the 1970s. Turning more towards power ballads without abandoning their hard-rocking base, Aerosmith conquered the music and video charts."

And the Rock and Roll Hall of Fame recognized the group's longevity:

> **"Meanwhile, their canon of great music and reputation as an unbeatable live act continues to grow. Perhaps most notably, the same five musicians who came together as Aerosmith in 1970 are still together more than 30 years later, as their train keeps a-rolling with no end in sight."**

Back on Tour and a New Album

The *Just Push Play* tour ended in early 2002. During the tour, the VH1 program *Behind the Music* recorded performance and interview segments for a two-hour special on Aerosmith. Once the tour was finished, the remaining segments were recorded. Viewers had the chance to get an "up close and personal" look at Aerosmith and its individual members.

In July of 2002, Aerosmith released *Oh, Yeah! The Ultimate Aerosmith Hits*. The two-disc set was a history lesson of the band and its music. The group included a new single on the set, "Girls of Summer." The release of the single led to a short "Girls of Summer" Tour. Opening for Aerosmith were two other big names in music: Run-DMC and Kid Rock. This was the last tour for Jason "Jam Master Jay" Mizell. Not long after Run-DMC had fulfilled its obligations to the tour, he was murdered. As of early 2007, his murder remains unsolved.

More honors came to Aerosmith in 2002, when it was named the second MTV Icon (Janet Jackson was the first). The guys were interviewed about everything from their childhoods, to how they met, to their legendary drug use, to blueberry pie. According to Joey,

> **"The band is a democracy. I compare us a lot of times to a blueberry pie. If you take a slice of blueberry pie out of the pie and replace it with apple . . . APPLE! It doesn't work. How I can relate that to being a democracy is that we're all blueberries. We all work together in that if I have a question about something that I'm not real sure of about myself, I'll go to Tom to ask him, and I'm going to get an honest answer**

Aerosmith was back on tour in 2003, coheadlining a tour with KISS. But the group interrupted its tour schedule to perform at the NFL 2003 Kickoff Live Concert on the National Mall in Washington, D.C. This wasn't the group's first brush with professional football. In 2001, they performed at the Super Bowl halftime show.

from him because he knows me. Nothing is going to be held back. There's no person that's more important than the other when it comes to treating each other equally."

Though some of the comments might have seemed odd and perhaps more than a little difficult to understand, the interviews did give viewers a unique insight into the rock legends.

More Tours, More Music

In 2003, Aerosmith coheadlined a short tour of North American amphitheaters with another rock legend: KISS. For Aerosmith, the main purpose of the Rocksimus Maximus tour was to give audiences a sneak preview of some of the material that would be included on its upcoming album, *Honkin' on Bobo*.

Fans had waited a long time for *Honkin'*, but when the album was released in 2004, the result was worth the wait. For several years, the band had promised it would release a more bluesy album, one that reflected the early influences on the group. The timing of the album's release fell during a resurgence in interest in roots music.

Roots music is American folk music that served as the basis for later American music styles. Some of the styles classified as roots music are bluegrass, country, gospel, blues, Cajun, jug bands, and Appalachian folk. Rock 'n' roll, blues, and jazz are three of the genres that developed from those styles. *Honkin'*'s release took advantage of increased interest in the genre.

On March 11, 2004, Aerosmith took off on the *Honkin' on Bobo* tour. The group limited its concerts to the United States and Japan. This time, however, the band concentrated on smaller markets. Opening for Aerosmith during most of the tour was Cheap Trick. As had come to be expected, the tour met with enthusiastic—though smaller—audiences.

Still Recording, Still Touring

In October 2005, Aerosmith released *Rockin' the Joint*, a CD/DVD set. The day before Halloween, the group embarked on the tour in support of the album. This time, the first part of the tour concentrated on major cities in North America. Lenny Kravitz opened for the band at most of the venues. The group planned to focus on smaller markets during the spring 2006 leg of the tour. That part of the tour had to be canceled, however, when it was announced in March 2006 that Steven required surgery for a ruptured blood vessel in his throat.

Steven was back in full voice in time to perform with Joe at the annual Fourth of July concert held by the Boston Pops Orchestra. The group also announced its next tour: the Route of All Evil tour. This time, Mötley Crüe would open half the shows. But before

On Halloween Eve 2005, Aerosmith kicked off the *Rockin' the Joint* tour in support of its newly released CD/DVD set. On the first leg of the tour, Lenny Kravitz (shown in the center of this photo with Joe on the left and Steven on the right) would open for the band.

The 50 Greatest Boston Songs
BONUS: Free Local Music Downloads! Page 100

Boston

OCTOBER 2005

>The Legend That Is STEVEN TYLER...

The Voice
BY ANDREW CORSELLO

The Sex Symbol
BY AMANDA FORTINI

The Innovator
BY KARL IAGNEMMA

The Pop Icon
BY DAVE ITZKOFF

The Survivor
BY GREG LALAS

+

Home Design Special: Clean and Simple Renovations

Heavy Profits, Hidden Risks: Boston's Fat Surgery Boom

Rib Eating, Pig Racing, and Down-Home Fun: The Best of Redneck New England

The Grape Gurus Who Pour the City's Best Wines

Steven has come a long way from Toxic Twin to sober rock icon. The October 2005 issue of *Boston* magazine featured Steven on the cover and an in-depth article. The article discussed his distinctive voice, his role as a music innovator, his image as a sex symbol and icon, and Steven the survivor.

the tour could begin, Aerosmith announced that Tom had been diagnosed with throat cancer and would have to miss the first half of the tour. David Hull, who had been part of Joe's Joe Perry Project filled in on bass.

In April 2007, Aerosmith began World Tour '07 with a concert in Brazil. The tour took the group to South America for the first time in fourteen years. Some countries in Europe would be able to see the group in person for the first time in eight years. Other countries would have the opportunity to see Aerosmith for the first time. Among the countries the group scheduled for its world tour were Mexico, the United States, the United Arab Emirates, Denmark, Sweden, Germany, Russia, Latvia, India, Estonia, Italy, Ireland, France, Belgium, and England. Aerosmith also expected to release an album in late 2007.

As busy as Aerosmith has kept Steven and Joe, they have made time for individual projects as well.

Steven on His Own

Unlike Joe, Steven has had no time apart from Aerosmith. He did make time to sing "Rockin' on Top of the World" for the 2004 film *The Polar Express.* He also sang the lead on Santana's "Just Feel Better" in 2005.

Steven's talents expanded into acting as well. In 2002, he played Santa on the hit children's television show *Lizzie McGuire,* and in 2005, he had a cameo appearance in *Be Cool.* Fans of the CBS television series *Two and a Half Men* were treated to Steven's performance playing himself as Charlie's loud neighbor.

In 2003, Steven received an honorary degree from the Berklee College of Music. In 2005, the University of Massachusetts in Boston awarded the Aerosmith frontman with an honorary doctorate. Steven's humanitarian side came out in 2006 when he served Thanksgiving dinner to the poor in Florida before an Aerosmith concert.

Steven has had health issues as well. In the early 1980s, he collapsed during a performance. In 2006, he needed surgery to treat a throat problem. Steven also disclosed in 2006 that he had been treated for hepatitis C for three years, but as of his statement, was free from the disease. Hepatitis C is a viral blood infection that can lead to liver disease. Although Steven did not disclose how he contracted the sometimes-fatal disease, one common method of transmission is the use of infected needles. Steven has made education about the disease one of the purposes of his life. In his statement, he said:

> **"Hepatitis C is the one that, of all the people in this room, at least three have it and don't know about it. It's the silent killer. I may go on Oprah and talk about this."**

Aerosmith has been on top of the rock world for many years, something that most groups envy but can't match. And it doesn't look as though the group will stop performing anytime soon. The band has also influenced other groups, including Nirvana, Van Halen, Bon Jovi, and Metallica. That's part of what makes Aerosmith a rock legend.

Joe on His Own

Joe had one hit album with the Joe Perry Project, during his "break" from Aerosmith. In 2005, he released his first solo album, *Joe Perry*. He played all of the instruments on the tracks except for the drums. To those who thought he could only play the guitar, this came as quite a surprise. The album was a commercial and critical success. He was nominated for a 2006 Grammy for Best Rock Instrumental for "Mercy," but lost out to guitar legend Les Paul.

But music isn't Joe's only talent. Joe has also earned a reputation as a chef. He has his own line of hot sauces, Joe Perry's Rock Your World Hot Sauces. The sauces are available in many supermarkets as well as on their own Web site, www.joeperrysrockyourworld.com. Joe's cooking talents were also featured on an episode of Rachael Ray's *Inside Dish* on the Food Network.

Along with Brad, Tom, and Joey, Steven and Joe have been part of one of the most influential bands in rock history. Groups including Nirvana, Metallica, Van Halen, Bon Jovi, Pearl Jam, and Stone Temple Pilots credit Aerosmith with influencing their music. Steven is proud of the influence Aerosmith has had on rock music.

"It's cool when I meet young guys from other bands who say how much an impact Aerosmith has had on them and how much they like me. I'll give 'em that 'C'mon you don't mean that' routine, but in my heart I know where they're coming from."

No one can argue with the success or influence of Aerosmith. It's what makes them a legend.

1969   Steven Tyler meets Joe Perry and Tom Hamilton.

1970   Aerosmith is formed.

1971   Brad Whitford joins the group.

1972   The group signs its first recording contract.

1973   The group releases its first album.

1974   Aerosmith has the first of a series of hit albums.

1975   "Sweet Emotion" becomes the group's first top-40 hit.

1976   Aerosmith begins its first headlining tour.

1977   The group tours Japan for the first time.

1978   Aerosmith appears in the Beatles' film *Sgt. Pepper's Lonely Heart's Club Band*.

   Live! Bootleg receives critical and commercial success.

   July 4 The group headlines Texas Jam '78 Festival.

   October 3 Aerosmith bails out fifty-three fan who had been arrested for smoking marijuana at a concert.

   October 10 Steven and Joe receive injuries when a concertgoer throws a cherry bomb on the stage at a show in Philadelphia.

1979   Joe Tyler leaves the group.

1980   Aerosmith's *Greatest Hits* album is released and the group finds commercial success again.

   Steven is seriously injured in a motorcycle accident.

1981   Brad Whitford leaves the group.

1984   Joe and Brad return to the group.

   June 22 The Back in the Saddle reunion tour kicks off.

1985   Joe and Steven kick their drug habits.

   November The reunited Aerosmith releases its first album.

1986   Steven and Joe sing on Run-DMC's remake of "Walk This Way."

1987 All members of Aerosmith successfully complete rehab programs.

Permanent Vacation becomes the group's best-selling album in ten years.

1990 "Janie's Got a Gun" wins the group's first Grammy Award.

1993 *Get a Grip* becomes the group's first album to debut at #1.

The group wins a Grammy Award for "Livin' on the Edge."

1994 "Crazy" wins a Grammy Award.

1998 "I Don't Want to Miss a Thing" becomes one of the group's biggest hits ever.

1998 "Pink" wins a Grammy Award.

1999 Aerosmith works with Disney to become an amusement park ride.

2001 *Just Push Play* is released.

January Aerosmith performs at the halftime show at the Super Bowl.

March Aerosmith is inducted into the Rock and Roll Hall of Fame.

October Aerosmith performs at the United We Stand: What More Can I Give: A Concert for America.

2002 Aerosmith is named an MTV Icon.

2004 *Honkin' on Bobo* is released.

2006 The group announces that Tom is being treated for throat cancer.

March Steven is treated for a throat problem. He also announces that he has been treated for hepatitis C.

2007 **April** Aerosmith embarks on World Tour '07.

Albums

1973 *Aerosmith*
1974 *Get Your Wings*
1975 *Toys in the Attic*
1976 *Rocks*
1977 *Draw the Line*
1978 *Live! Bootleg*
1979 *Night in the Ruts*
1980 *Greatest Hits*
1982 *Rock in a Hard Place*
1985 *Done with Mirrors*
1986 *Classics Live!*
1987 *Classics Live! Vol. 2*
    Permanent Vacation
1988 *Gems*
1989 *Pump*
1991 *Pandora's Box*
1993 *Get a Grip*
1994 *Big Ones*
    Box of Fire
1997 *Nine Lives*
1998 *A Little South of Sanity*
2001 *Just Push Play*
    Young Lust: The Aerosmith Anthology
2002 *O, Yeah! The Ultimate Aerosmith Hits*
2004 *Honkin' on Bobo*
2005 *Rockin' the Joint*
2006 *Devil's Got a New Disguise*

Number-One Singles

1989 "Love in an Elevator"
1990 "The Other Side"
    "What It Takes"
1993 "Cryin'"
    "Livin' on the Edge"
1994 "Deuces Are Wild"
1997 "Falling in Love (Is Hard on the Knees)
    "Pink"
1998 "I Don't Want to Miss a Thing"
2001 "Jaded"

Select Videos

1987 *Aerosmith's Video Scrapbook*
1988 *3 X 5*
1989 *Things that Go Pump in the Night*
1994 *Big Ones You Can Look At*
2002 *Just Play Japan*
2004 *You Gotta Move*
2006 *Permanent Vacation*

Book

2003 Aerosmith and Stephen Davis. *Walk This Way: The Autobiography of Aerosmith.* New York: HarperEntertainment.

Select Awards and Recognition

1990 American Music Award: Favorite Artist—Heavy Metal/Hard Rock; Grammy Award: Best Rock Performance by a Duo or Group with Vocal ("Janie's Got a Gun"); *Billboard* Music Award: Rock Album Artist; MTV Video Music Award: Best Rock Video (*Janie's Got a Gun*).

1991 MTV Video Music Award: Best Rock Video (*The Other Side*).

1993 American Music Award: Favorite Pop/Rock Band, Duo, or Group and Favorite Heavy Metal Artist; Grammy Award: Best Rock Performance by a Duo or Group with Vocal ("Livin' on the Edge").

1994 *Billboard* Music Award: #1 Rock Artist; Grammy Award: Best Rock Performance by a Duo or Group with Vocal ("Crazy"); MTV Video Music Award: Best Video of the Year (*Cryin'*).

1999 *Billboard* Music Award: Artist Achievement Award; Grammy Award: Best Rock Performance by a Duo or Group with Vocal ("Pink").

2000 American Music Award: International Artist Award.

2001 Aerosmith is inducted into the Rock and Roll Hall of Fame.

2002 Aerosmith is named an MTV Icon.

2004 *Rolling Stone* ranks Aerosmith #57 on its list of the 100 Greatest Artists of All Time.

Books

Aerosmith and Stephen Davis. *Walk This Way: The Autobiography of Aerosmith.* New York: HarperEntertainment, 2003.

Anjou, Erik. *Aerosmith.* New York: Chelsea House, 2002.

Bowler, Dave, and Bryan Dray. *Aerosmith: What It Takes.* Chicago, Ill.: Trafalgar Square, 1997.

Dome, Malcolm, and Carrie Meback McGovern. *Aerosmith: Life in the Fast Lane.* New York: Viking, 1994.

Foxe, Tyler, Cyrinda, and Danny Fields. *Dream On: Livin' on the Edge With Steven Tyler and Aerosmith.* New York: Berkley Boulevard, 2000.

Web Sites

www.aeroforceone.com
Aerosmith Official Fan Club

www.aerosmith.com
Aerosmith Official Site

www.aerosmith.net
Aerosmith Sony Site

www.aerosmith-lyrics.com
Aerosmith . . . Nuthin' but the Lyrics

www.joeperrymusic.com
Joe Perry

www.joeperrysrockyourworld
Joe Perry's Rock Your World

www.rockhall.com
Rock and Roll Hall of Fame

blues—A style of music that developed from African American folk songs in the early twentieth century, consisting mainly of slow sad songs often performed over a repeating harmony.

cover—To record a new version of a song first performed or made popular by another artist.

criteria—Accepted standards used in making decisions or judgments about something.

derivative—Copied from somewhere and not original.

double entendres—Remarks that can be taken more than one way, one of them usually sexually suggestive.

induction—The act of installing someone formally into an office or group.

jam—To play music in an improvised way, often in a group.

oblivion—A condition of forgetting everything or of being unaware of surroundings.

platinum—A signification that an album or CD has sold one million copies.

precipice—A high, vertical, or very steep cliff.

prestigious—Having a distinguished reputation.

psychedelic rock—A style of rock music that tries to replicate the effects of mind-altering drugs.

punk—A type of rock music characterized by confrontational lyrics that reflect the punk youth movement of the 1970s.

rite of passage—An event or act that marks a significant transition in a human life.

venues—Performance locations.

Ethan Schlesinger is a freelance author. He lives in Upstate New York.

Picture Credits

page

2: Geffen Records/Star Photos
8: UPI Photo Service
11: AFP Photo/Stan Honda
12: KRT/MCT
14: Columbia Records/NMI
17: Rex Features
18: New Millennium Images
20: Columbia Records/NMI
22: Foto Features Collection
25: Rex Features
26: Photo Trend Int'l
29: Rex Features
30: Star Photo Archive

32: Columbia Records/PRPS
35: Photo Trend Int'l
37: Star Photos
38: Photo Trend Int'l
40: UPI Photo Archive
41: Sony Music/KRT
42: Star Max Photos
44: Geffen Records/KRT
47: UPI Newspictures
49: Abaca Press/KRT
51: Splash News
52: New Millennium Images
54: Newswire Photo Service

Front cover: Geffen Records/Star Photos